Take It Easy,
Charlie Brown

Charles M. Schulz

Selected Cartoons from
You'll Flip, Charlie Brown, Vol. 2

CORONET BOOKS
Hodder Fawcett, London

Copyright © 1965, 1966, 1967 by
United Feature Syndicate, Inc.

First published by
Fawcett Publications Inc., New York 1973

Coronet edition 1973
Sixth impression 1978

Printed in Great Britain for Hodder
Fawcett Ltd., Mill Road, Dunton Green,
Sevenoaks, Kent (Editorial Office:
47 Bedford Square, London, WC1 3DP) by
C. Nicholls & Company Ltd.,
The Philips Park Press, Manchester

ISBN 0 340 17844 2

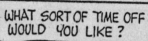

➤

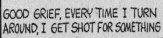

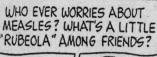

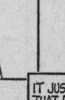

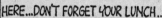

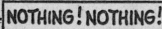

GOOD GRIEF! IT SNOWED LAST NIGHT!

SO HERE I AM COVERED BY A SOFT BLANKET OF SNOW... I THINK I'LL LEAP UP AND SCATTER IT IN ALL DIRECTIONS...

➡

→

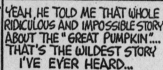

TRICKS OR TREATS!

→

RATS!

NEW YEAR'S DAY AND WHERE AM I? ALONE IN A STRANGE COUNTRY.. WHAT IRONY!

HOW MUCH LONGER CAN THIS WAR GO ON? IF IT DOESN'T END SOON, I THINK I SHALL GO MAD!

GARÇON, ANOTHER ROOT BEER, PLEASE

HOW MANY ROOT BEERS CAN A MAN DRINK? HOW MANY DOES IT TAKE TO DRIVE THE AGONY FROM YOUR BRAIN? CURSE THIS WAR! CURSE THE MUD AND THE RAIN!

→

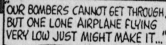

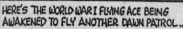
HERE'S THE WORLD WAR I FLYING ACE BEING AWAKENED TO FLY ANOTHER DAWN PATROL...

HERE'S THE WORLD WAR I FLYING ACE WALKING OUT ONTO THE FIELD...

IT SNOWED LAST NIGHT... BUT TODAY THE SUN IS OUT...THE SKY IS CLEAR..

I CLIMB INTO THE COCKPIT OF MY SOPWITH CAMEL...

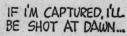

THEY'RE RIGHT...
IT IS A LONG WAY
TO TIPPERARY!

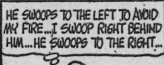

AH! HE HIT IT RIGHT. TO MY SHORTSTOP! THIS'LL BE AN EASY OUT...

HERE'S THE WORLD WAR I FLYING ACE ZOOMING THROUGH THE AIR IN HIS SOPWITH CAMEL..

❋ SIGH ❋

SCHULZ

© 1970 United Feature Syndicate, Inc.

Wherever Paperbacks Are Sold

FOR THE LOVE OF PEANUTS

☐ 02710 X	For the Love Of Peanuts (2)	50p
☐ 04409 8	Who Do You Think You Are,	
	Charlie Brown (4)	50p
☐ 04305 9	Fun With Peanuts (5)	50p
☐ 04295 8	Here Comes Snoopy (6)	50p
☐ 04318 0	You're My Hero, Charlie Brown (7)	50p
☐ 04406 3	This Is Your Life, Charlie Brown (8)	50p
☐ 04294 X	Let's Face It, Charlie Brown (9)	50p
☐ 04407 1	Slide Charlie Brown Slide (10)	50p
☐ 10788 X	Good Grief, Charlie Brown (12)	50p
☐ 10595 X	Here's To You, Charlie Brown (13)	50p
☐ 10541 0	Nobody's Perfect, Charlie Brown (14)	50p
☐ 10673 5	Very Funny, Charlie Brown (15)	50p
☐ 10761 8	Hey, Peanuts (17)	50p
☐ 12614 0	You're Too Much, Charlie Brown (21)	50p
☐ 12618 3	Here Comes Charlie Brown (22)	50p
☐ 12543 8	The Wonderful World of Peanuts (24)	50p
☐ 12544 6	What Next, Charlie Brown? (26)	50p
☐ 15828 X	Have It Your Way, Charlie Brown (29)	50p
☐ 17322 X	You're Something Special, Snoopy (33)	50p
☐ 12838 0	You're a Brave Man Charlie Brown (18)	50p
☐ 12786 4	We Love You, Snoopy (19)	50p
☐ 12521 7	You've Done it Again, Charlie Brown (23)	
		60p

All these books are available at your local bookshop or newsagent, or can be ordered direct from the publisher. Just tick the titles you want and fill in the form below.
Prices and availability subject to change without notice.

CORONET BOOKS, P.O. Box 11, Falmouth, Cornwall.
Please send cheque or postal order, and allow the following for postage and packing:
U.K. – One book 22p plus 10p per copy for each additional book ordered, up to a maximum of 82p.
B.F.P.O. and EIRE – 22p for the first book plus 10p per copy for the next 6 books, thereafter 4p per book.
OTHER OVERSEAS CUSTOMERS – 30p for the first book and 10p per copy for each additional book.

Name...

Address...

....